POLYMER CLAY
FOR BEG

Book 1 - Millefiori Canes

By
Sue Heaser

INTRODUCTION

This little book is the result of over 20 years of teaching polymer clay. While publishers have kept me busy writing full length books, I have always felt a need for a small manual that would help beginners get started and give them all the basic knowledge in one place. Millefiori or flower caning is probably the most popular technique that beginners want to master so that is what I have concentrated on here. I hope you will enjoy taking your first steps in polymer clay as much as I enjoy teaching beginners!

Sue

Copyright © 2013 Sue Heaser

Photography by Sue Heaser

All rights reserved.

CONTENTS

Polymer Clay	4
Tools and Equipment	5
Jewellery findings	7
Basic Techniques	9
Mixing colours	10
Baking	11
Finishing and gluing	12
Jewellery assembly	13
Making blends	16
Flower canes	20
Leaf canes	24
Millefiori pendant	26
Millefiori beads	28
Natasha beads	30
Cane slice jewellery	32
Earrings	34
Suppliers and websites	36
Index	38

POLYMER CLAY

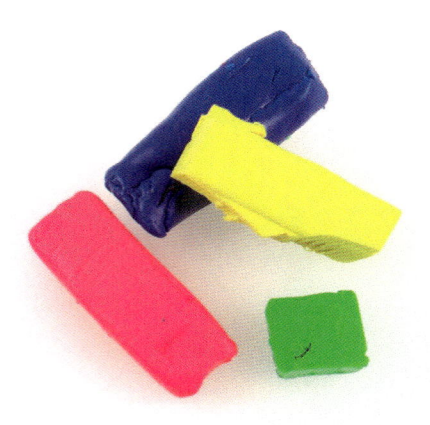

Polymer Clay is a highly versatile modelling material that is hardened by baking in the home oven. Once baked it is permanent and can be cut, sawn, glued, painted or added to and re-baked. It comes under the brand names of Fimo, Premo Sculpey, Cernit, Kato Clay and Pardo clay to name some of those most widely available.

Polymer clay is sold in small packages of 2 ounces (56 grams) and also in larger sizes. The small size packs are ideal for beginners and all the projects in this book need less than a package. The packages of clay are available in a wide range of colours and these can be mixed together to make further colours. Most brands also produce a "transparent" or translucent clay which can be used on its own or mixed with colours to make delicate translucent pastel shades. There is also night-glow, gorgeous pearl and metallic clays, stone effect clays and fluorescent clays.

TOOLS AND EQUIPMENT

Most equipment will be at hand in your own home. The following items are the basic tools you will need when starting with polymer clay. As you gain experience, you may want to add to these but my favourite tools are the following and you can do everything in this little book with them:

A work surface. A smooth melamine chopping board is ideal, or else a ceramic tile or a cutting mat.

Craft Knife. A curved blade like the one shown is the most versatile.

Slicer blades. Also called tissue blades, these long straight blades are invaluable for slicing millefiori canes and cutting straight edges on sheets of clay.

Rolling tools. A small acrylic or nylon rolling pin is the best type or you can improvise with a small bottle or jam jar. For even rolling, place two strips of thick card on either side of the clay as you roll it out. A pasta machine is not essential but is great fun and speeds up rolling and conditioning. It can also be used to make blends and larger sheets of clay which are used for millefiori caning.

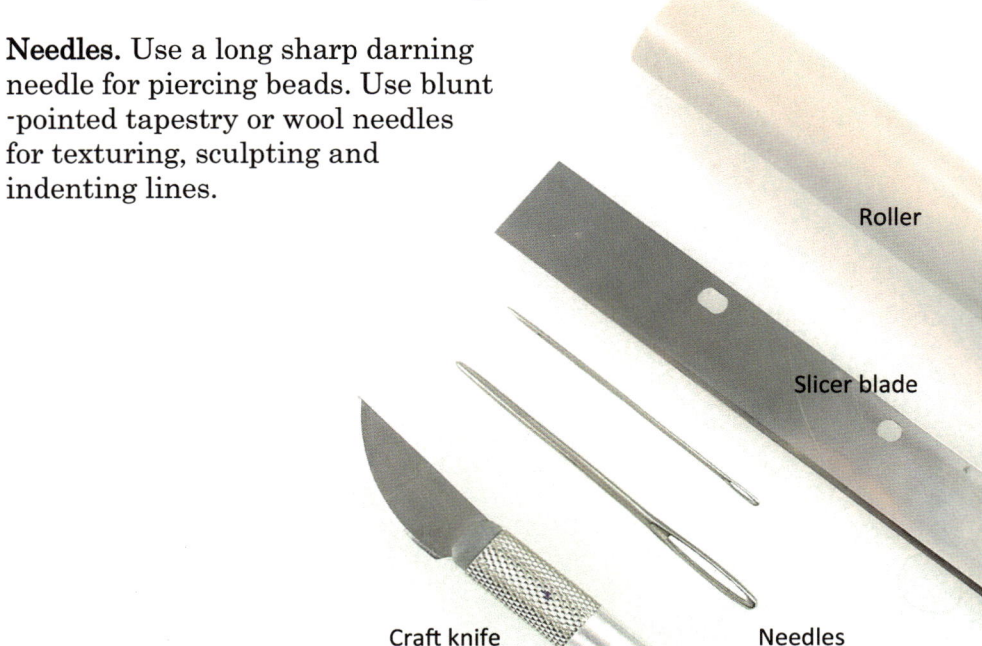

Needles. Use a long sharp darning needle for piercing beads. Use blunt-pointed tapestry or wool needles for texturing, sculpting and indenting lines.

Roller

Slicer blade

Craft knife

Needles

Baking sheet (Cookie sheet). Covered with non-stick baking parchment or ordinary paper for baking the clay.

Ceramic tile. Use for making flat-backed pieces that can be rolled out, shaped, and then baked on the tile without moving them.

Cookie cutters. These are available in a wonderful range of shapes and sizes from simple geometric circles and squares through to more exotic motifs. Find them in kitchen supply stores or from polymer clay and metal clay suppliers.

Wet Wipes. For cleaning hands and work surfaces.

Oven. Your home oven is fine for baking polymer clay. A fan oven is ideal or any electric oven. Gas ovens and ranges such as Agas should be used with an oven thermometer to check the temperature.

Canes slices and beads ready for assembly into jewellery

JEWELLERY FINDINGS

Jewellery findings are the pieces of metal that are used to connect polymer clay creations to the body. Silver or gold plated findings are widely available and economical to buy. The most useful findings for beginners include the following:

Eyepins and Headpins
Long pins with a loop or a head which have many uses. They can be embedded in the clay to form an attachment point or threaded through beads after baking to make pendants or dangling earrings. They come in different lengths.

Headpins and eyepins

Brooch backs
These are glued to the flat back of a polymer clay piece to make brooches.

Jump rings
Small wire rings used to link pieces of jewellery or attach findings.

Brooch backs

Necklace clasps
There is a large variety available from simple hooks to those with a spring such as lobster claws. Magnetic clasps are becoming very popular too.

Jump rings

Ear hooks or Ear Wires
Used for making dangling earrings.

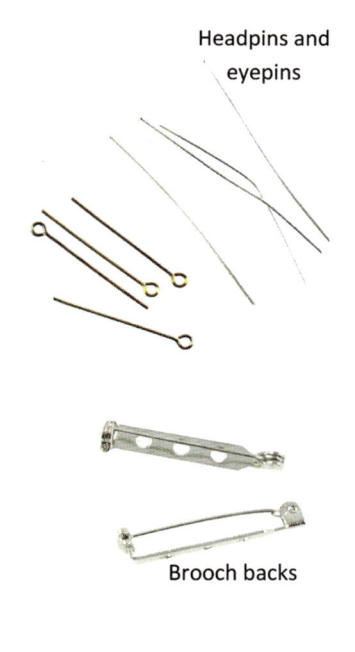

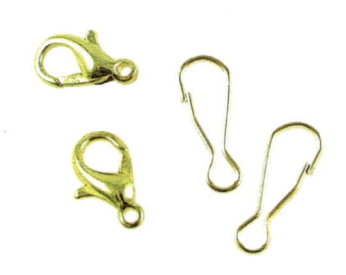

Ear wires

Necklace clasps

7

Spring ends
These are squeezed onto the end of cotton cord and leather thong to finish a necklace and provide an attachment point for the clasp

Thong and Cord
There are many kinds available. Waxed cotton cord or leather thong 2mm thick works well with polymer clay jewellery.

Spring ends for cord

Pliers and Wire cutters
You will need fine nosed pliers for attaching findings. Round nosed are used for making neat loops while snipe nosed are for general purpose wire work and for opening and closing jump rings and loops. If you only buy one pair, the round nosed will do most jobs. Wire cutters are used to trim head pins or wire - some pliers have integral cutters.

Pliers: round nosed and snipe nosed

BASIC TECHNIQUES
WORKING WITH POLYMER CLAY

Conditioning the clay
Always work each piece of polymer clay in your hands before use to soften it. Cut a piece off the block and roll it into a log, fold the log in half and roll again. Repeat until the clay folds easily without cracking. Some clays require more working than others. You can also use a pasta machine to condition your clay by cutting a thin slice from the block of clay and then passing it through the pasta machine on its widest setting. Fold in half and roll through again, continuing until the clay is soft and flexible.

If the clay is too soft
Press a rolled out sheet of clay between two sheets of ordinary white paper and leave for a few hours or overnight so that some of the oily plasticizer leaches out.

If the clay is too stiff
Soften hard clay by kneading in a few drops of Sculpey Clay Softener or mixing with Fimo Mix Quick.

It is not necessary to squash pieces together hard to effect a join as they will fuse together when baked; gentle but firm pressure is all that is needed. Fingernail marks and dirty fingerprints on light colours will ruin your results so keep your hands clean, wiping them with wet wipes between colours if necessary.

SAFETY
Polymer clay is very safe to use and has a non-toxic label world wide. It is safe to bake in your home oven and for children to use. Avoid burning the clay which will happen if your oven rises over about 340° F / 170°C. Like any burning plastic, the smoke smells unpleasant and should not be inhaled. If this happens, turn off the oven and ventilate the room well.

MIXING CLAY COLOURS

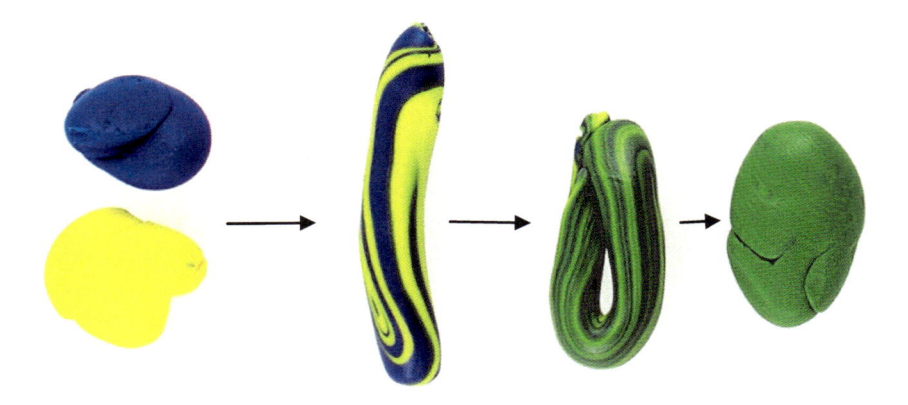

Polymer clay colours can be mixed together to make new colours. Soften the two colours you want to mix first and then work them together, folding and rolling until all the streaks have disappeared.

When making pastel colours, add only a very small quantity of colour to white: about 1 part colour to 8 parts white. If you roll both colours into equal diameter logs, it is easier to estimate the quantities. e.g. 1cm colour to 8cms white. (Or 1/2in to 4in.) Alternatively you can roll out a sheet of each clay colour and use a cutter to cut out the relevant number required of each colour to mix.

You can mix most colours from a basic palette of blue, yellow and magenta or crimson red, plus black and white. Translucent clay can be tinted with small quantities of Coloured clay.

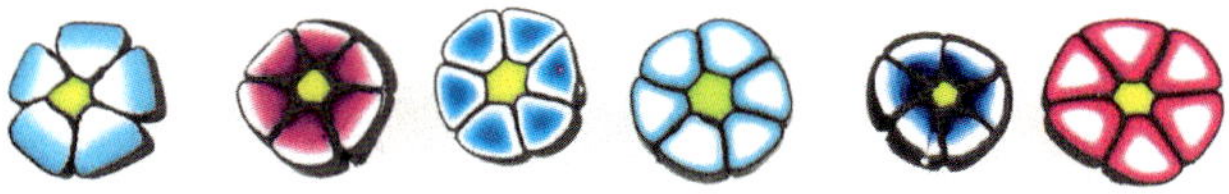

BAKING POLYMER CLAY

Polymer clays should be baked in the oven on a baking sheet lined with paper or baking parchment for about 20 minutes to 1 hour at 275°F / 130° C. Some brands have different baking requirements so follow the directions on the pack.

To bake your polymer clay creations, lay a sheet of baking parchment on a metal baking sheet and place the clay pieces on the paper. Alternatively, you can make pieces on a ceramic tile and place them on the tile directly in the oven. Bake for the time recommended and then remove from the oven and cool. The clay will not harden until completely cool.

Clay that has not been baked long enough will be fragile and break easily. Items can be re-baked repeatedly without harm and fresh clay can be added to a baked piece and then baked again.

Beware of overheating the clay by letting the oven temperature go too high as it gives off toxic fumes when burnt. If you have problems with baking, your oven thermostat may not be accurate so check with a simple test bake: Form some test strips of clay, 1/16in (1.5mm) thick, 1/2in (13mm) wide and about 2in (5cms) long. Bake and cool. The pieces should bend into a U bend at least 5 times without breaking. If they snap easily, turn your oven up 10° and re-bake. If they show signs of discolouring, turn your oven down 10°.

FINISHING POLYMER CLAY

Polymer clay jewellery does not need any finishing after baking and the clay surface has a pleasing satin texture. However, if you wish you can finish your pieces in a variety of ways:

Varnish: Use a water based acrylic gloss varnish to make your pieces shiny. Do not use varnishes that contain solvent or white spirit because these do not dry properly on polymer clay. You should always varnish pieces that have been coated with pearlescent powders or the powder may wear off.

Paint: You can paint baked polymer clay using acrylic paints. Degrease the surface by brushing with alcohol or meths first so that the paint sticks. Do not use enamel or oil paints which do not dry properly on baked clay.

Sanding: You can sand your pieces with fine wet and dry sandpaper or sanding sponges to give them a lovely glassy shine but it is hard work! Buff with a piece of quilt wadding or denim to bring up the shine after sanding.

GLUING POLYMER CLAY

Polymer clay is not compatible with some glues but all the following work well:

Superglue: this works well with polymer clay and is used to glue baked pieces together or to mend any breakages. It can also be used to attach findings to baked clay

Epoxy glue: two part epoxy glues such as jeweller's epoxy and araldite are the best glues to use for attaching jewellery findings to baked polymer clay because they are so durable.

PVA glue: White craft glue is the glue to use to attach polymer clay to fabrics or absorbent materials such as wood. Use PVA glue as a key, brushed thinly onto baked polymer clay when adding fresh clay. Let it dry and then add the fresh clay. It is also used to attach soft clay to glass or metal when covering a piece with cane slices.

JEWELLERY ASSEMBLY

You will need to learn some simple techniques for turning your polymer clay canes and beads into wearable jewellery. Basic techniques are given here while the individual projects have more specific information.

USING JUMP RINGS

Jump rings have many uses in jewellery. They are used as connections between different elements, to add dangles, attach eyepins to earrings and many other uses. Use a jump ring to attach a cord or chain to a polymer clay pendant that has been pierced with a simple hole.

Use a jump ring that is large enough to go through the thickness of the baked clay and allow room for a cord or chain to be threaded through it. Open the jump ring by pushing the two ends sideways as shown - not by pulling them apart. This makes it easier to return the jump ring to a complete ring when closing it. Use pliers for this - two pairs give you more leverage but you can use one pair and push against your finger, or another tool if the jump ring is stiff. Thread the jump ring through the hole in the clay and push the two ends back together with your pliers.

MAKING A CORD NECKLACE

Cord necklaces are some of the simplest to make and are ideal for polymer clay jewellery. Attach a large jump ring to polymer clay pendants or beads and thread on a cord. There are many different types of cord available from waxed cotton cord to leather thong and various silk and rubber cords.

Materials
- Cord - 18in (50cm) length or as required - 2mm thick
- Two spring ends for 2mm cord
- Necklace clasp
- Pliers

1. Push a spring end onto one end of the cord. Use your pliers to squeeze the last coil of the spring end firmly onto the cord to secure it. Tug the cord to make sure it is firm.

2. Repeat for the other end of the cord. Attach a necklace clasp to one of the spring end loops. The second spring end loop makes a firm connecting point for the clasp.

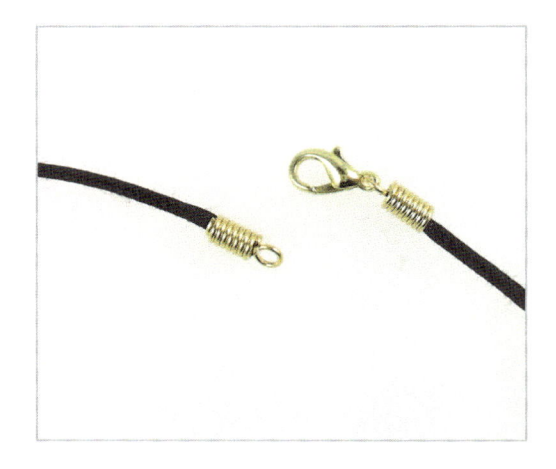

MAKING MILLEFIORI CANES

Canes are logs of clay with a pattern running through the centre rather like a stick of rock or holiday candy. They can be sliced up to make beautiful repeating patterns. "Millefiori" means a thousand flowers and is term borrowed from glass-making which is used to describe these canes.

Many different kinds of canes can be made using polymer clay but flower and leaf designs are some of the easiest for beginners to make and the following pages show you how to make these popular canes.

MAKING A BLEND

A blend is a gradient from one colour to another within the clay and If you enjoy caning, learning how to make a blend will add wonders to your work. This is a simple way of making what is widely known as a Skinner Blend. The steps here show how to make a blend using a simple roller; a pasta machine can be used instead and speeds up making blends considerably.

1. Use a 1/4 of a 2oz (56g) block of clay in each of two contrasting colours. Shape each into a tall triangle and roll them both flat. They should be about 1/4in (6mm) thick. Do not worry about making them neat and regular - rough edges do not matter at this stage.

2. Lay the flattened triangles together as shown and slightly overlapping. Roll them with your roller to flatten further into a rectangular sheet about 1/8in (3mm) thick. Again, rough edges do not matter at the moment but you can trim any really ragged edges.

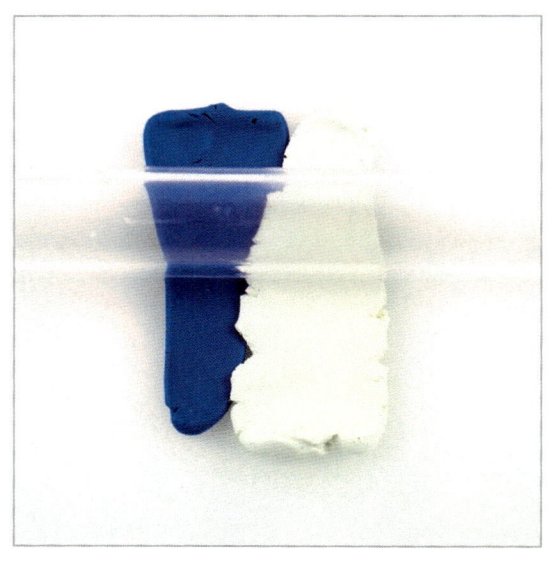

3. Fold the sheet in half towards you, so that one side is all white and the other is all blue. Keep this orientation throughout the subsequent rolling. Roll the piece again to the original thickness.

4. Continue folding and rolling flat, always folding the same way. After a while, the central area of the clay will become streaky as the overlapping colours in the centre mix. Continue and they will smooth out into a continuous gradient.

5. The finished blend. Now roll it thinner to stretch it across the colours to make the blend more spread out. It should be about 1/32in (1mm) thick.

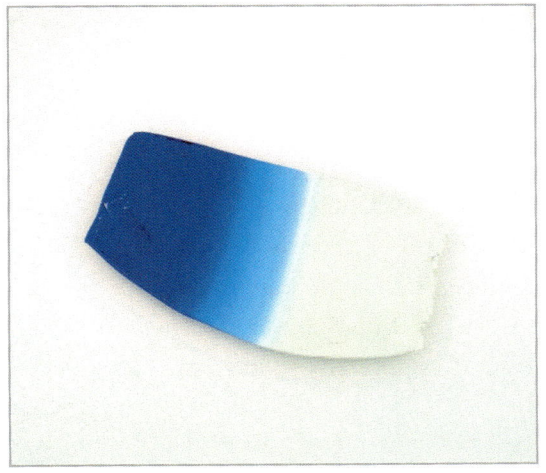

6. For a cane with a light centre, start rolling it up at the light end. For a dark centre, roll from the dark end. Take care to make the first roll tight to exclude air.

7. The finished rolled blend grading from light in the centre to dark on the outside. This is used in the instructions on page 20 to make a flower cane. You can make blends that grade more gently by making your original triangles wider.

8. Another way of using the blended sheet is to make a graded loaf blend. I call this a "flip-flop": Start from the dark end of the sheet and fold the sheet in 1/2in (13mm) folds alternately one way then the other to create a concertina effect for a loaf that grades from light to dark from top to bottom.

9. The finished loaf cane. This can be used to make the petal cane for a flower cane in the same way as the round cane on page 20. Wrap it in black in the same way and pinch the point along either the light or the dark side.

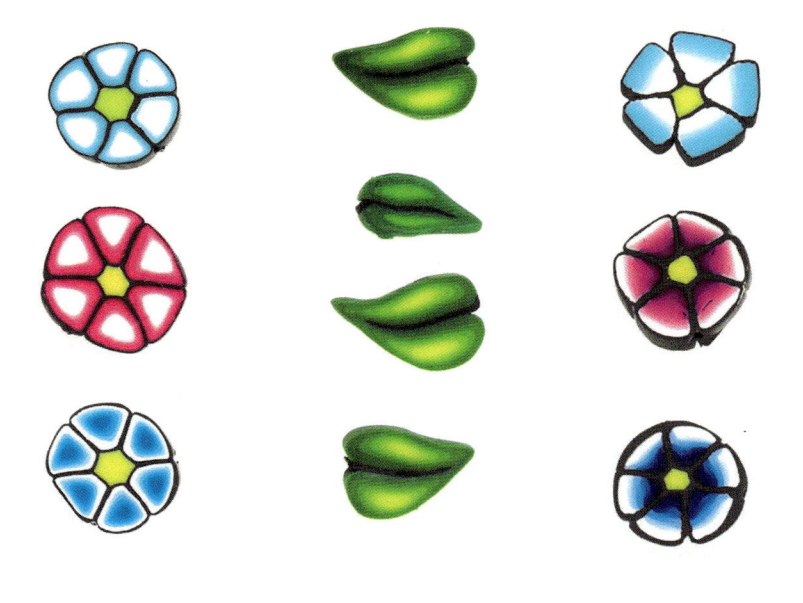

Flowers made from
rolled blends

Leaves made from
rolled blends

Flowers made from
loaf blends

19

FLOWER CANES

These steps show the simplest type of flower cane. Once you have mastered the techniques, you can experiment with many different colours and shapes.

1. Use a blended log about 3in (7cm) long and 3/4in (20mm) thick (see page 16). Alternatively you can use a log of plain colour for an easier flower.

2. Roll out a thin sheet of black clay, about 1/32in (1mm) thick. Trim the side towards you and lay the cane on the edge. Trim the other two sides to match the cane.

3. Roll the cane up in the black sheet. When the first edge touches the black sheet, trim the sheet and smooth it round the cane to make a butt joint.

4. Roll the cane into a long log, about 12in (30cm) long. Cut off the distorted ends and cut the rest into 6 equal pieces. It is easier to do this if you lay the log along a ruler.

5. Pinch along the top of each length to give it a triangular cross section. These will be the petals of the flower. The pointed tops will be placed towards the centre of the flower.

6. Roll out a log of yellow clay about 3/16in (5mm) thick and trim to the same length as the petal sections. This will be the yellow centre of the flower. You can use a different colour if you wish but yellow is such a common flower centre colour it always looks good.

7. Now start building the cane. Lay the yellow log along the pointed top of one of the petal sections. Press another petal section next to it and then a third. This should give you half a flower in cross-section.

8. Fit the remaining three section into the flower, always making sure that the pointed part of the petal touches the yellow log all along its length. Check the other end of the cane as well to make sure all is accurately placed.

9. Press the parts of the cane together to consolidate them, squeezing the cane all along its length. If the clay is soft enough, you can pull the cane to lengthen it, otherwise, roll it on your work surface to elongate it.

10. When the cane is about double the original length and 1/2in (13mm) thick, cut it in half to see the results. It is best to always use canes from the centre outwards - the ends will be distorted.

Slicing a cane: Let the cane rest to cool and become firmer. Use a sharp blade to cut thin slices from your cane about 1/32in (1mm) thick for applying to beads and backgrounds. Rotate the cane a quarter turn between each slice to prevent squashing it.

To make smaller flowers, roll a section of the cane to elongate it further and reduce the cross-section size. This is called "reducing" a cane. You can make flowers of many different sizes.

LEAF CANES

These are easy canes to make and go beautifully with flower canes. Try pinching the cross-section into different shapes for variety.

1. Make a blend using green and golden yellow. To make a realistic leaf green mix together one part brown clay with three or more parts of bright green. (See colour mixing on page 10.)

2. Roll up the blended sheet with the yellow in the middle and then roll the resulting log to elongate to about 4in (10cm) long. Cut it in half to make two 2in (50mm) lengths.

3. Press each half down on your work surface so it has a semi-circular cross-section. Roll out a thin sheet of black clay and press the flattened side of one half of the green log onto it. Trim all round the black sheet to fit the log.

4. Press the flat side of the second green log onto the black sheet. This will make a black line down the centre of the leaf for a midrib. Trim any black sheet that protrudes out of the cane.

5. Roll or pull the cane to lengthen it to about 6in (15cm) long. Pinch one side of the cane into a point all along its length so that the cross-section becomes leaf shaped. Cut the cane in half to reveal the leaf. It is now ready for slicing. Reduce further if you want smaller leaves.

USING CANES: MILLEFIORI PENDANT

Cane slices can be used for all kinds of jewellery from decorating beads to applying slices to plain background shapes as shown here. I have used a 2in (50mm) diameter round cutter for the basic shape but you could try using a different shape as you wish.

1. Roll a sheet of black clay, 1/8in (3mm) thick and lay it on a tile. Cut out a shape with a cookie cutter. Press down firmly with the cutter until it hits the tile and then move it slightly from side to side to ensure it has fully cut out the shape.

2. Pull away the waste clay from around the shape and leave the shape on the tile for decorating with cane slices. This means that your pendant will not get distorted by removing it from the tile.

3. Cut slices from a leaf cane and arrange on the cut-out shape. Do not press the slices down until you have added them all so you can re-arrange if you wish.

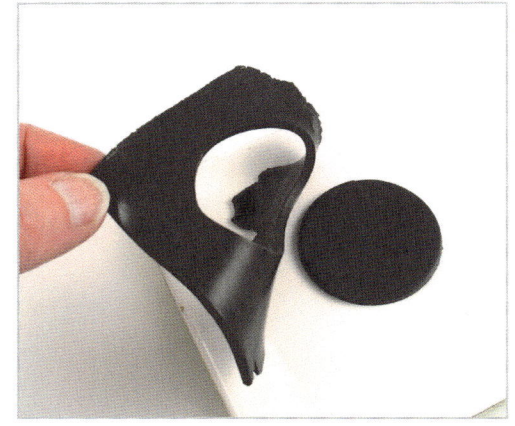

4. Now cut slices from different flower canes - large and small look good put together. Arrange these to cover the base of the leaves. You can make a symmetrical pattern - or asymmetrical - the choice is yours.

5. Use a large wool needle to make a hole about 1/8in (3mm) in from the edge for hanging. The hole should be large enough to take a jump ring for hanging. Bake the piece on the tile. When cool, remove it from the tile. If it has stuck to the tile during baking, slide a blade carefully between the clay and the tile to free it.

6. Attach a large jump ring through the hole (see page 13) and thread on a cord or leather thong. Try making pendants in lots of different colours and shapes.

27

MILLEFIORI BEADS

Rolling balls of clay for beads is easy to do and you can decorate your beads with repeating patterns of flowers and leaves using slices from your canes. Black or white clay shows up flower canes well but you can use any colour you like. The bead shown at the right has been threaded on a head pin with contrasting glass beads to make a pendant.

1. Condition a lump of clay about 1/2in (13mm) diameter and roll into a ball by rotating it in your hands. Cut thin slices from your flower and leaf canes and press them lightly onto the surface of the clay ball, arranging them so that they are attractively spaced.

2. Now roll the ball again between your hands and the cane slices will sink into the clay surface until no join is visible.

3. Place the ball on your work surface and use a sharp darning needle to pierce straight down the centre of the ball. Lift the ball on the needle and twist the needle right through the clay.

4. Roll the bead back and forth on your palm to smooth the clay surface, make the bead round again after piercing and to enlarge the hole.

Place the bead, hole vertical, on a tile or piece of paper laid on a baking sheet and bake. See page 33 and 35 for ideas on how to make a bracelet or earrings using your beads.

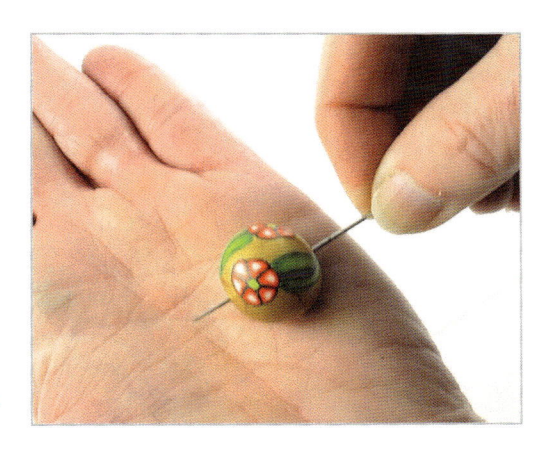

Tip: After baking, if the hole is too small for your chosen threading material, twist a small drill bit in the hole to enlarge it.

29

NATASHA BEADS

These clever beads use up the scrap ends of canes - so you never waste anything! Partly mixed clay is shaped into a bead and cut open - the bead is in effect turned inside out.

1. Select clay with contrasting colours and push the pieces together into a 3/4in (20mm) ball. Roll the ball into a log and fold in half, repeating about four times to slightly mix the clay.

2. Shape the clay into a rectangular cube by pressing it down on your work surface on all sides. Make it as even as possible which will make the next steps easier. Now cut straight down the centre with a blade. Remove the blade carefully from the clay.

3. Pull the two halves apart carefully to reveal the pattern inside and then push them together again side by side, matching the two symmetrical parts of the pattern.

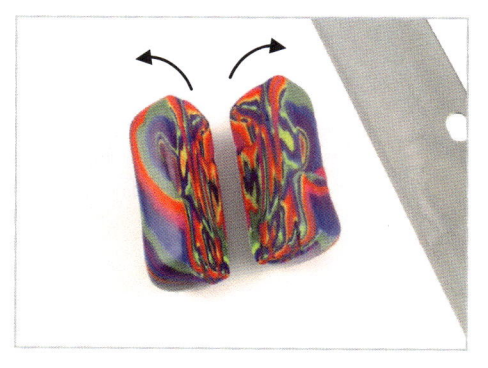

4. The two sides will match perfectly. You can now pierce the top to make a pendant or continue to make a bead. Make sure that you get the pattern matched perfectly - precision gives a professional finish to your work.

5. Make another vertical cut exactly half way between the centre cut and each side edge. Pull out the pieces as before - each will reveal another matching pattern. Flip each quarter round the back, matching the pattern and press in place.

6. The finished bead with the outer two pieces pressed into place. The final side will also have a matched pattern. Pierce through the centre and bake. Thread on a head pin and turn a loop for attaching with a jump ring to a thong (see page 35).

CANE SLICE JEWELLERY

Cane slices can be used to make beads in their own right. Thread them on headpins for dangling earrings or glue them onto ear stud pads or clips. Threaded on elastic cord, they make lovely bracelets.

1. Cut the cane slices about 1/8in (3mm) thick so that they are thick enough to pierce horizontally. Use a sharp darning needle to push a hole right through the cane horizontally. Twist the needle as you push to make it enter the clay more easily.

2. If the needle emerges in the wrong place, pull it back a little and push it through again. You can heal the hole that was made in the wrong place by smoothing with a fingernail. Sometimes the clay will split where you make the hole - just smooth over to make it join up again.

3. Leaf canes can be pierced at an angle to make them hang more naturally. Lay the cane slices flat and bake - the holes will not fill up. After baking, if the hole is not big enough for your chosen threading material, enlarge it by twisting a fine drill bit (1mm is ideal) through the hole. You do not need a drill.

BRACELETS

To make a bracelet, thread the slices on elastic cord such as Stretch Magic. Tie the ends firmly in a double knot and add a touch of superglue to secure.

You can use beads instead for a beaded bracelet - or a mixture of slices and beads.

EARRINGS

Thread cane slices and beads onto headpins to make pretty dangle earrings.

Materials:
- Two matching cane slices or beads
- Two fish hook ear wires
- Small glass beads of a toning or contrasting colour
- Two headpins
- Wire cutters and round nosed pliers

1. Thread some glass beads onto the head pin, then thread on a cane slice. Thread on some more beads of your choice. Black beads offset bright colours well or you can choose toning colours to match the cane slices.

2. Trim the headpin wire to 1/4in (6mm) above the top bead with your wire cutters. Hold the beads firmly down onto the head of the headpin and push the wire over at a right angle just above the top bead.

3. Grip the end of the wire in the jaws of round nosed pliers and turn a loop back towards the beads until it is centred over the emerging wire. You can make different sized loops in this way by altering how far up the plier jaws you grip the end of the wire.

4. Open the loop on the bottom of an ear wire by pushing it sideways with your pliers (see "Using Jump Rings" on page 13). Thread on the loop made in the top of the headpin and close the ear wire loop.

Bead Earrings: Beads decorated with cane slices are threaded on headpins and finished in the same way. These beads have been decorated with small cane slices patted on and not rolled in so they are raised from the surface of the bead.

35

SUPPLIERS

Polymer clay is available in art and craft shops throughout the world. Alternatively there are many mail order suppliers on the web. Search on "polymer clay" or on the brand of your choice. The following are recommended mail order suppliers:

UK SUPPLIERS

www.clayaround.co.uk

www.georgeweil.co.uk

www.polymerclay.co.uk

US SUPPLIERS

www.polymerclayexpress

www.clayfactory.net

AUSTRALIAN SUPPLIERS

www.polymerclay.com.au

NEW ZEALAND SUPPLIERS

www.zigzag.co.nz

Findings, beads and cords are available from beading and jewellery making suppliers. Many advertise in jewellery making magazines.

USEFUL WEBSITES

Sue Heaser: www.sueheaser.com
(Information about Sue's books and workshops; free polymer clay projects; resources and suppliers for tools and materials used in her books.)

British Polymer Clay Guild: www.bpcg.org.uk

International Polymer Clay Guild (USA): www.theipca.org

Polymer Clay Daily: www.polymerclaydaily.com
(Daily updates of work in polymer clay worldwide)

Polymer Clay Central: www.polymerclaycentral.com
(Many tutorials, swaps, ideas, huge archive)

Sculpey website: www.sculpey.com
(Lots of free projects)

Polymer clay forum: www.polyclay.co.uk

Also check Yahoo groups - several polymer clay groups. Search on polymer clay: http://groups.yahoo.com

INDEX

Baking	11	Jump rings	7
Baking sheet (Cookie sheet)	6	Jump rings, attaching	13
Basic techniques	9	Leaf cane	24
Blend, loaf	18	Loop, making	35
Blend, rolled	18	Milefiori pendant	26
Blends	16	Millefiori beads	28
Bracelets	33	Millefiori canes, making	15
Brooch backs	7	Natasha beads	30
Cane slice jewellery	32	Necklace clasps	7
Cane, reducing	23	Necklace, making	14
Cane, slicing	23	Needles	5
Ceramic tile	6	Oven	6
Clay, conditioning	9	Paint	12
Clay, working with	9	Pliers	8
Colours, mixing	10	Polymer clay	4
Cookie cutters	6	Rolling tools	5
Cookie sheet	6	Safety	9
Cord	8	Sanding	12
Craft knife	5	Slicer blades	5
Cutting out	26	Spring ends	8
Ear hooks	7	Suppliers	36
Ear wires	7	Thong	8
Earrings	34	Tile	6
Eyepins	7	Tissue (Slicer) blades	5
Flower cane	20	Tools	5
Gluing	12	Varnish	12
Headpins	7	Websites	37
Introduction	2	Wet wipes	6
Jewellery findings	7	Work surface	5

7623432R00023

Printed in Great Britain
by Amazon.co.uk, Ltd.,
Marston Gate.